Fire TV Stick Made Easy

A Comprehensive Step-by-Step User Guide

for Amazon's Fire TV Stick

Edward Jones

"Fire TV Stick Made Easy" © 2 December 2014 by Jones-Mack Technology Services of Charlotte, NC (print edition).

Digital rights provided by agreement to Amazon Digital Services, Inc. Print rights provided by agreement to CreateSpace, an Amazon company.

Amazon, Fire TV Stick, Fire TV, Kindle, Kindle Fire, the Amazon Kindle logo and the Kindle Fire logo are trademarks of Amazon.com, Inc. or its affiliates. All other trademarks mentioned are the property of their owners. The author of this book is in no way associated with any products described or mentioned throughout this book.

No part of this book may be reproduced, stored within a retrieval system, or transmitted without the express permission of the publisher. All rights reserved.

Contents

Chapter 1 - Introducing Fire TV Stick 7
About this book 8
What's under the hood 8
How Fire TV Stick compares to the competition 9
Gaming 10
Amazon Fire TV Stick vs. Amazon Fire TV 12

Chapter 2 - Getting started with Fire TV Stick 15
Fire TV Stick Setup 17
Connecting Fire TV Stick to the Internet 18
Fire TV Stick registration 19

Chapter 3 - Selecting and Viewing Content 21
Fire TV Stick Basics Video by Amazon 21
Main menu navigation 23
Accessing your content 26
Removing content from your Fire TV library 29
Using voice search to find content 30
Installing Netflix 31
Mirroring your Kindle Fire to your Big-Screen TV 33
Using the Parental Controls feature of Fire TV Stick 34
Installing and Using the Fire TV Remote App 35
About Amazon Prime & Amazon Prime Instant Video . 38
To buy or not to buy, that is the question 40
The Murky Practice of 'Geo-dodging' 41

Coming soon: Amazon FreeTime for Fire TV Stick 44

Chapter 4 -Playing games with Fire TV Stick 47

    Which Controller? 49

    Pairing additional Game Controllers 50

    Playing games 51

    Navigating with the Game Controller 51

    Uninstalling games 52

    About Amazon GameCircle 53

        Changing your GameCircle Profile 56

        Hiding Your GameCircle Profile 56

    Ten Games worth considering for Fire TV Stick 56

    Fibbage, by Jackbox Games 57

    You Don't Know Jack, by Jackbox Games 58

    Flappy Bird, by Dotgears 59

    Zen Pinball HD, by Zen Studios 60

    Tetris, by Tetris Online, Inc. 61

    Monsters University by Disney 63

    Sonic the Hedgehog 2 by SEGA 64

    Bingo Blitz by Buffalo Studios, LLC 65

    The Game of LIFE by Electronic Arts 67

    Despicable Me: Minion Rush by Gameloft 68

Chapter 5 - Apps you should have in your Fire TV library 71

    1. Netflix 73

    2. Hulu Plus 75

    3. Crackle 77

    4. Pandora 79

5. iHeart Radio 81

  6. Showtime Anytime 82

  7. Movies by Flixter 83

  8. Plex 84

  9. WatchESPN 85

  10. Bloomberg TV 86

  11. VEVO 87

  12. TuneIn Radio 88

  13. Frequency 89

  14. HuffPost Live 90

  15. Red Bull TV 91

  16. RealPlayer Cloud 92

  17. Vimeo by Vimeo 94

  18. Portfolio for OneDrive by Snapwood Apps 95

  19. tinyCam Monitor Pro for IP Cam 96

  20. YouTube 97

Chapter 6 - It's your life: photos, personal videos, and music 99

  Installing Amazon Cloud Drive on your computer, tablet, or smartphone 99

  Viewing your photos and videos 101

  Organizing your photos into albums 102

  Creating slideshows and screensavers 102

  Playing music from your Music Library 103

Chapter 7 - Sideloading Apps 105

  Downloaading and installing apps by sideloading 106

So, where's my app? 108

Where do I find apps worth sideloading? 109

Chapter 8 - Basic troubleshooting tips for Amazon Fire TV Stick 111

Amazon Fire TV Stick Troubleshooting Help Video 113

CONCLUSION (and a favor to ask!) 115

Chapter 1 - Introducing Fire TV Stick

If you are reading this book, you've already acquired, or are very interested in, Amazon Fire TV Stick. For those who are in the second category and may be wondering what the excitement is all about, Amazon Fire TV Stick is a tiny yet powerful streaming media device, roughly the size of a USB flash drive, that connects to the HDMI connector of your TV set and uses the power of the Internet to bring an unmatched range of entertainment into your home.

(Artwork courtesy Amazon, Inc. unless otherwise noted.)

Fire TV Stick is a stunningly simple, low-cost way to watch entertainment from all of the popular streaming services- Netflix, Amazon Prime Instant Video, Hulu plus, Showtime, Crackle, and more, along with low-cost video rentals. Add to this the ability to play games, the ability to run a variety of apps, and the ability to display photos and personal videos that you've stored in the Amazon Cloud, and you have a feature set that adds up to a hard-to-beat combination in the world of streaming media delivery.

With this user guide, you'll learn everything you need to know about Fire TV Stick, from the basics involving set up and ways to access your streaming content to advanced topics that include mirroring between Fire TV and a Kindle Fire tablet, and ways to show photos you've stored in the Amazon Cloud as a slideshow using your Fire TV Stick.

About this book

In addition to serving as a tutorial that will quickly get you up to speed on the use of Fire TV Stick, this book also serves as a source of tips, tricks, and traps for using your Fire TV Stick. Interspersed throughout nearly all chapters of this book, you will find three categories: *tips*, *tricks*, **and** *traps*. *Tips* are techniques that make things easier in terms of use, in a particular area. *Tricks* are techniques that change the operation of your Kindle Fire in a particular area. And *traps* are "gotchas," things to watch out for, that can cause problems.

What's under the hood

Amazon Fire TV Stick is, as of this writing, the most high-powered streaming "stick" device available. Under the hood is a high-performance dual-core Qualcomm processor with four times the processing power of the Roku streaming stick, four times the memory capacity of Google's Chromecast, and 32 times the memory of the Roku streaming stick. The following serious hardware can be found under the hood of the Fire TV Stick:

- Qualcomm dual-core processor
- VideoCore4 dedicated graphics processor
- 1 GB of RAM
- 8 GB of internal flash memory based storage
- Dual band dual Wi-Fi antenna for faster streaming and fewer dropped connections

- Support for Dolby Digital surround sound
- Output resolution of 720 pixel and 1080 pixel, up to 60 frames per second
- An exclusive feature called ASAP (Advanced Streaming and Prediction) predicts which movies and TV shows you are likely to watch, and buffers them so you will see playback quickly. The technology overcomes the problem of long load times that plague streaming competitors like Apple TV.

How Fire TV Stick compares to the competition

For consumers, the world of streaming media in the home is just getting started, but that's not preventing consumers from jumping into the marketplace. The desire to vastly increase viewing options and to reduce ever-growing cable TV and satellite TV charges has been an irresistible draw for many. Currently, there are four major players in the consumer marketplace: Apple TV, Google Chromecast, Roku, and Amazon's Fire TV product line which includes Fire TV Stick.

In terms of both features and costs, Fire TV Stick is in the same overall price range as are two of its three competitors: the low-end model of the Roku media streaming device, and Google's Chromecast. Both are also priced under $50 at the time of this writing. Fire TV Stick compares admirably when a feature-for-feature comparison is made, as is shown in the following chart.

fireTVstick	Fire TV Stick	Google Chromecast	Roku Streaming Stick
List Price	$39	$35	$49
Features			
Remote Included	✓		✓
Processor	Dual-core	Single-core	Single-core
Memory	1 GB	512 MB	512 MB
Flash Storage	8 GB	2 GB	256 MB
Dolby Digital Plus certified surround sound	✓		
Wi-Fi	Dual band/Dual antenna (MIMO)	Single band	Dual band/Dual antenna (MIMO)
Voice Search	Remote app; voice remote sold separately		
HDMI extender included	✓	✓	
HDMI video out (up to 1080p)	✓	✓	✓
Popular Services			
Netflix	✓	✓	✓
Amazon Instant Video	✓		✓
Hulu Plus	✓	✓	✓
YouTube	✓	✓	✓
Pandora	✓	✓	✓
PBS Kids	✓	✓	✓
WatchESPN	✓	✓	✓
Bloomberg TV	✓		✓
Crackle	✓	✓	✓
Twitch	✓	✓	
HBO GO		✓	✓
Games			
Number of Games	Over 200	Less than 30	Less than 100
Optional dedicated game controller (sold separately)	✓		

(Chart courtesy Amazon, Inc.)

Gaming

As another portion of the Fire TV Stick feature set, Amazon has integrated support for video gaming within the Fire TV product line. The dual-core Qualcomm processor that powers Fire TV Stick combined with the VideoCore4 dedicated graphics processor makes for responsive graphics. The hardware's gaming features have been combined with gaming software: high quality, low-cost games like **You Don't Know Jack, Monsters University, Sonic the Hedgehog 2, The Game of Life, Flappy Birds Family**, and many others. As an added bonus, this is gaming software that will not break the family budget, with games costing an average of less than two dollars per game (many games are free). Hundreds of games are available at the time of this writing, with more on the way.

 In addition to using the Fire TV Stick remote to play games, you can also choose to use the optional Amazon Fire TV game controller, enabling more high-intensity and complex gaming with its dual analog sticks and complete assortment of controls.

Amazon Fire TV Stick vs. Amazon Fire TV

Fire TV stick isn't the only offering in the streaming marketplace to come from Amazon. The company also sells Amazon Fire TV, a set top console that provides access to streaming media. If you are still considering a buy decision, you may be wondering about the difference between the two offerings.

The price difference-- under $40 for the Fire Stick, just under $100 for Amazon Fire TV-- implies a greater feature set for the higher priced offering. For the extra money, Fire TV provides a quad core processor (compared to the dual-core processor in the Fire Stick), twice the memory of the Fire Stick, and support for wired Ethernet. Fire TV also includes a search by voice feature; this feature is available as an option with Fire TV Stick. Due to its greatly increased processing power, Fire TV is a superior platform for high-performance games. If a family member is into gaming, you will probably be much better off spending the extra dollars on a Fire TV rather than the Fire TV Stick.

For those who have already made that "buy" decision, if you are the proud owner of a Fire TV Stick, read on. You're about to discover multiple ways in which you can exponentially increase the entertainment experience within your home.

Chapter 2 - Getting started with Fire TV Stick

From a hardware standpoint, Fire TV Stick packs a significant combination of technology into a clean and simple design. Out-of-the-box, you see just five items, plus a printed 'quick-start' guide: the Fire TV Stick itself, the handheld remote control, a power adapter with a matching USB cable, an HDMI extender, and a set of AAA batteries (to power the remote control). The following illustration shows the hardware that is in the box when your Amazon Fire TV Stick arrives.

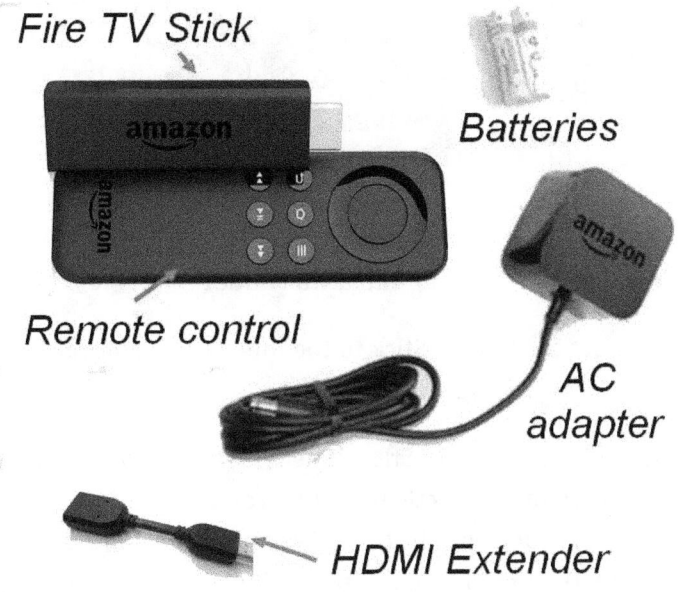

Set up of an Amazon Fire TV Stick is deceptively simple, and basically involves the following four steps:

1. Connect the Fire TV Stick to the power adapter, and to an HDMI port on your TV set. When connecting the stick to the HDMI port of your TV, Amazon recommends that you use the HDMI Extender for better Wi-Fi reception.

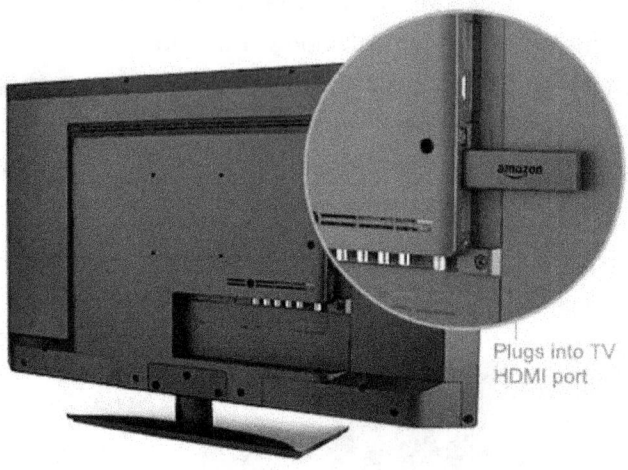

2. Insert the AC adapter into a wall outlet

3. Connect the Fire TV Stick to the Internet by entering your Wi-Fi password when asked.

4. Register your Fire TV Stick, if necessary. (If you ordered your Fire TV Stick directly from Amazon using your Amazon account, registration will not be necessary, as your Fire TV Stick will be registered for you automatically.)

While you are getting familiar with Fire TV Stick, note the various buttons on the remote control (see illustration)-

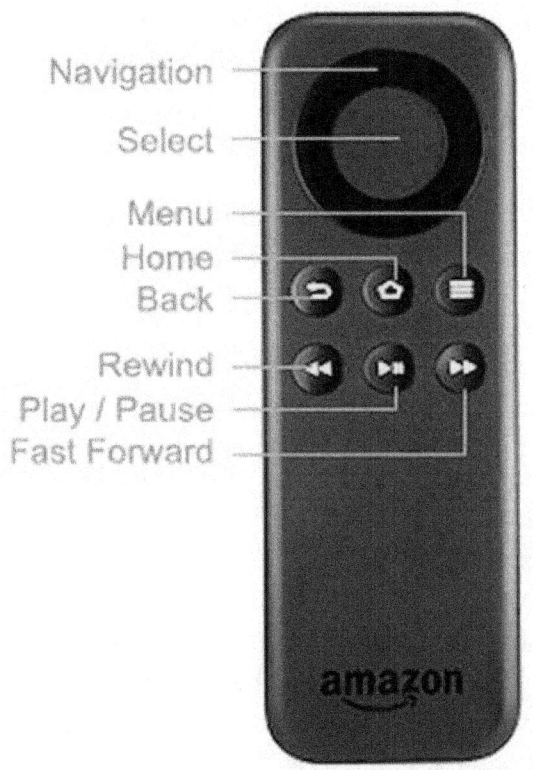

The Fire TV Stick remote is at the heart of the process of choosing your content, and the chapter that follows will cover this topic in detail.

Fire TV Stick Setup

1. Connect your Fire TV Stick to your TV set. As a first step, connect the silver ("plug") end of the Fire Stick to an HDMI connector on your television set. When connecting the stick to the HDMI port of your TV, Amazon recommends that you use the HDMI Extender for better Wi-Fi reception.

NOTE: If your TV set is connected to a home entertainment receiver with its own HDMI input connectors, you should connect the silver ("plug") end of the Fire Stick to the receivers HDMI input jack.)

2. Connect the AC Adapter cable to the matching connector on your Fire TV Stick, and insert the adapter plug into a wall outlet.

3. Turn on your TV set, and set your TV set's input selector to the HDMI input that is connected to the Fire TV Stick.

4. Install the batteries supplied with your Fire TV Stick into the battery compartment of the remote control. Included with your Fire TV Stick is a set of AAA batteries that must be installed in the remote. Examine the rear of the remote and locate the small clip at one end of the battery cover door. Pull on this clip to remove the battery cover, and insert the batteries into the remote, following the directions printed inside the remote's rear cover. Finally, re-insert the rear cover on the remote control.

5. Press and hold the Home button on the Fire TV Stick remote for five seconds, then release.

6. Follow the on-screen directions that appear on your TV screen to complete your Fire TV Stick setup.

Connecting Fire TV Stick to the Internet

You'll need to connect Fire TV Stick to the Internet, by means of a wireless ("Wi-Fi") connection to your home network. Shortly after you turn on your TV with the Fire Stick installed and powered up for the first time, you will see a screen appear that asks how you wish to connect to the Internet. You'll be presented with a list of wireless networks that are within range of your Fire TV Stick. Using the circular trackpad at the center of the Fire Stick remote, highlight your home network by name on the screen, and press the round button inside the circular trackpad to select your network.

2. At the next screen that appears, enter your network password (assuming yours is a secured network).

Your Fire Stick will automatically detect the presence of an Ethernet connection, and will download the most recent updates to its operating system. (This may take anywhere from 1 to 10 minutes, depending on the speed of your Internet connection.)

Fire TV Stick registration

If you ordered your Fire TV Stick using your Amazon account, the device has been preregistered for you. If you received your Fire TV Stick as a gift or purchased it from a retailer, simply follow the on-screen directions that appear after you setup your Internet connection to register the device.

Chapter 3 - Selecting and Viewing Content

The heart of all your available content in Fire TV Stick appears on the Fire TV Home Screen, which is the display that you see when you initially switch your TV to the appropriate HDMI input and press the home button on the Fire TV Stick remote. The following illustration shows a typical Fire TV Home Screen; yours will differ slightly, depending on which content you recently added, which content has been recently added to Amazon Prime, and which movies, games, and apps you may have added to your own Fire TV library.

Fire TV Stick Basics Video by Amazon

If you are a newcomer to Fire TV Stick, it's worth your time to watch Amazon's video covering basics, including the use of your Fire TV Stick remote. It will take perhaps five minutes of your time, and you can view the video at the Amazon web site. Point a web browser at www.amazon.com/help and at the page that appears, click "Fire, Kindle and Echo" on the left, then click "Fire TV Stick" on the right. At the next screen, under "Fire TV Basics," click "Fire TV Help Videos."

To navigate around your Home Screen and select content, you'll need to use the Fire TV remote control. As you may recall from the getting started chapter, your remote contains a circular Navigation trackpad you can use to move left, right, up, and down. In the center of the trackpad, you'll find the select button for choosing content that you highlighted on the screen. (The illustration that follows shows the layout of controls on the remote.)

Beneath the circular trackpad, you'll find a back button, a home button, and a menu button. You can press the back button repeatedly, to move back in a series of steps. The home button will return you to the Fire TV Home Screen from any point. The menu button will display a menu of various options, depending on what content, game, or app you are using at the time.

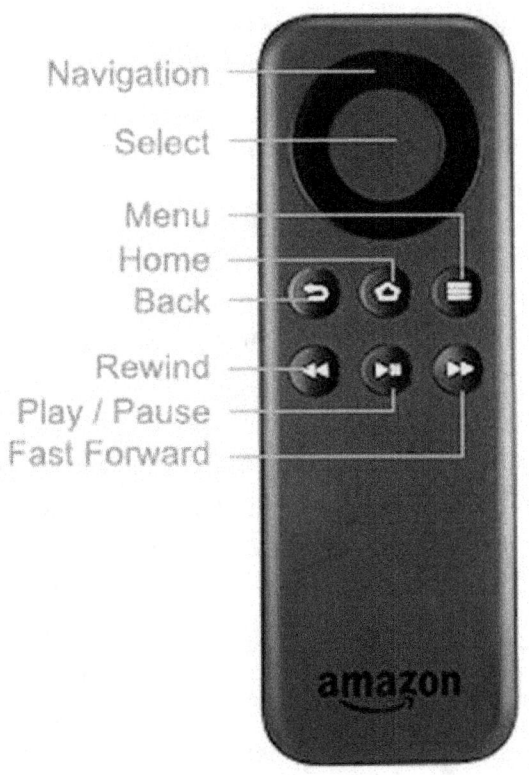

Main menu navigation

Press the Home button to get to the Home Screen, and at the left side of the screen, you will see the main menu. Use the up-and-down portions of the circular trackpad to highlight a main menu option, and press the select button in the center of the ring to choose that option. Here are your main menu choices in detail:

Search: Use the search option to search for movies, TV programs, games, apps, as well as music videos provided by Vevo. You search using an on-screen keyboard that appears when you select this option. (If you have purchased the optional Amazon Fire TV Voice Remote, you can use the innovative voice search feature that's built into your remote. However, note that voice search will search Amazon-supplied content, but does not currently search within apps like Netflix.)

Home: When Home is highlighted within the main menu, you can review your content recommendations as well as your recent activity. The Recent category will display movies, TV shows, games, or apps that you have recently viewed or used. The Featured movies and TV category will display content from Amazon and additional content providers. The Recommended movies and TV category shows a list of content that Fire TV recommends, based on your viewing habits. As you watch various movies and TV using Fire TV Stick, the system learns from your viewing habits and makes personalized recommendations based on your viewing taste. Additional movies, TV shows, apps, and games appear under a number of headings in this area that include 'Featured movies and TV,' 'Recommended movies and TV,' 'Shop new release movies,' 'Top movies on Prime,' and 'Top free apps and games.' The content that you see in these areas are based on automated listings compiled from what's most popular among Amazon Fire TV viewers.

Tip: Your recent content which appears at the top row of your Home Screen can become fairly cluttered as you use your Fire TV Stick. You can remove any item that appears in the recent category in order to reduce the amount of clutter. To do this, highlight any unwanted items in the recent category, then select Remove from Recent just beneath the highlighted item.

Movies: Use this option to rent or buy movies which can then be viewed from the Amazon Instant Video store. Note that Amazon Prime members can view any content in the Prime Instant Video library at no additional cost. (There are a number of benefits to being a member of Amazon Prime, and thousands of free movies is just one of those benefits; for more on this topic, see "About Amazon Prime and Amazon Instant Video" later in this chapter.)

TV: Use this option to rent or buy and watch TV shows also available from the Amazon Instant Video store. You can rent or buy individual shows, or you can buy the entire series for many popular shows. As with movies, Amazon Prime subscribers have access to thousands of TV shows at no additional cost.

Watchlist: The watchlist displays a list of movies and TV shows that you made a note of, and that you want to watch at a later time. As you browse among movies and TV shows in the Amazon Instant Library catalog, you'll see a button marked "add to watch list" under any given movie or TV show. You can navigate to and select that button to add that content to your watchlist as a reminder of something you'd like to view at a later time.

Video Library: Included in your video library, you'll find all of the instant video movies and TV shows that you have purchased or are presently renting. (Note this does not include movies and TV shows that you're watching using Prime Instant video.)

Games: Use this option to select and download games available from the Amazon App Store. If you are an avid gamer, you can also use this option to create a GameCircle profile that lets you view and compare your achievements and times played within a particular game.

Apps: Use this option to locate and download apps that are available from the Amazon App Store. With some apps, you will incur a cost to download the app, but many apps can be downloaded for free. Popular free apps include YouTube, Hulu plus, and Netflix. (See Chapter 5 for a listing of top-rated apps you may want to have in your Fire TV library.)

Music: Use the music option to play songs, artists, albums, or playlists that you have stored in the Amazon cloud. You can play music that you've obtained from the Amazon Music Store, or music that you've uploaded to the Amazon cloud.

Photos: Use the photos option to access any photos or videos that you stored in your Amazon Cloud Drive account. You can designate individual photos that are to be used as screensavers, and you can also launch photo slideshows that are based upon a collection of photos stored in your Amazon Cloud Drive.

Settings: Use this option to change the various settings for the behavior of your Fire TV Stick. The settings include parental controls, which can be used to block purchases, as well as to restrict access to movies, TV shows, games, apps, and photos.

Trap: Parental controls will not restrict content supplied by third-party apps. With third-party apps, it is up to the developer of the app to provide any parental controls.

Accessing your content

You can access a wide variety of content, both from Amazon and from a number of third-party vendors. There are different ways to access content, depending upon the type of content you are seeking.

With Fire TV Stick, your primary user interface-- that's "geek speak" for "how you get along with the device"-- is made up of two parts: a left side with selectable options, and a right side with content. As you scroll through each of the choices on the left, additional options on the right side are displayed.

In the illustration that follows, the left side shows Movies as the selected category on the left side, with "Recently added to Prime" as a chosen subcategory. A variety of movies that fall into this subcategory appear on the right side, directly beside the subcategory name.

To move deeper within a category, just press on the center of the circular trackpad. As you move deeper within the menu choices, options to play or purchase the content, game, or app will appear. To move back out of a category, just press the left side of the circular trackpad.

Keep in mind that you can also use the Back button on the remote to move back the way you came within the menu structure. And if you happen to lose your way, you can always move back to the Home Screen at any point, simply by pressing the Home button on the remote. You can use the steps noted below to access a given type of content on your Fire TV Stick.

To access this content:	Perform this step:
Prime instant video movies and TV shows:	Using the circular trackpad, navigate to the 'Top Prime movies or TV' listings or the 'Recently added to Prime movies and TV' listings. Select the icon representing the video that you wish to watch, and press the center select button on the remote.
Rentals or purchases from Amazon instant video:	At the Home Screen, select video library, then find the icon representing the movie or TV show you wish to watch and select it. (In the case of rentals, once the rental period has expired, you will no longer see the item available in your video library.)
Game purchases:	At the Home Screen, select games. When you do this, the games that you have purchased will appear in the Your Games Library. The listing that you see will include all games if you have purchased from the Amazon App Store.
Apps purchases:	From the Home Screen, select Apps. When you do this, all apps

	that you have purchased will appear in the Your Apps Library. (The library includes any and all apps that you purchased from the Amazon App Store.)

Tip: Mirror your Kindle Fire HDX to your TV screen using Fire TV Stick. If you own a Kindle Fire HDX, you can mirror whatever is displayed on your Kindle Fire to your TV set using Fire TV Stick. Before you do this, you need to make sure that the tablet and the Fire TV Stick are on the same WI-FI network. Then on the Kindle Fire HDX, drag down from the top of the screen and go to Settings > Display and sound > Display mirroring. In the window that appears, look in the Devices section, find the name of your Fire TV Stick, and tap it to begin mirroring.

Tip: if you are viewing a movie from Amazon Instant Video, you can use your Fire HD or Fire HDX as a second screen to display IMDb information about each scene. You can view character names, actor names and director names, and assorted trivia about the film that you are watching. To enable second screen, on Fire TV Stick, go to Settings > Second screen and make sure it is turned on. Once second screen has been turned on, you can also use the play / pause button and the location bar, both at the bottom of the screen of your Kindle Fire, to control the playback of Fire TV Stick.

Removing content from your Fire TV library

If you have items on your Home Screen that you are no longer viewing, you can remove these items to cut down on the visual clutter. Using the circular trackpad, navigate to the movie or TV show that you recently viewed, then select the 'Remove from recently watched' button that appears underneath. On your Home Screen, in the recent section, you will also see recommendations that have been personalized based on your recent use of Fire TV Stick. You can remove any items from this area by navigating to the item and then selecting the 'Remove from recent' button beneath.

Using voice search to find content

Amazon Fire TV Stick has an optional voice search feature that lets you search for a variety of content types, based on a spoken word or phrase. You can search movies or TV shows, and you can also search your games and apps libraries, as well as the Amazon App Store, for games or apps. **To use this feature, you must have the optional Voice Remote for Amazon Fire TV.**

To use the voice search feature, press and hold the voice button at the top of the Fire TV Voice Remote. A microphone icon will appear on your TV screen along with the word, "Listening..."

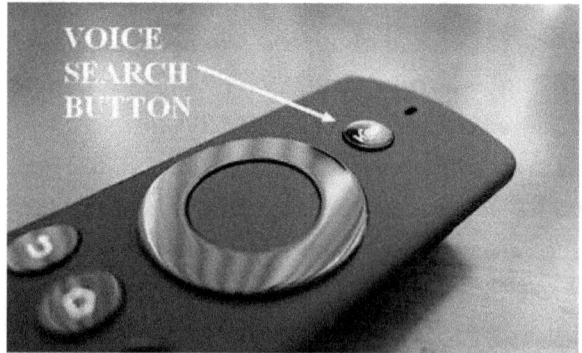

While holding the button depressed, say words related to the content you are seeking. You can say the name of a movie or TV show, an actor's name, a character name, or the name of a genre. Release the button and Fire TV will search the content library, the Amazon stores, and all compatible apps that may contain any related content. Once the search is complete, the search results will appear on the screen. You can then select the desired result within the list to view that content.

NOTE: While the Voice Search feature is impressive, note that it does have its limits (at least at the time of this writing). A major limitation of Voice Search is that it does not search third-party apps, and it does not search libraries other than Amazon's own Instant Video, and Hulu Plus. Voice search does NOT currently search Netflix. If you are a Netflix subscriber and Netflix has a movie you'd like to see (free to Netflix subscribers) and Amazon Instant Video has the same movie for $5.99, a voice search will find the Amazon title, but will ignore the Netflix title. (Netflix has stated that the company will support Amazon's voice search at a future time, so by the time that you read this, the problem may no longer exist.)

For best results with voice search, you should speak at a distance of 1 to 8 inches from the microphone, minimize background noise, and say a movie title, actor name, character name, or genre. You should NOT speak in complete sentences, as the voice search feature was not designed to deal with natural language processing.

Installing Netflix

Amazon Instant Video is certainly not the only possible choice when it comes to streaming video services; other popular choices include Netflix, Hulu, Crackle, and Wal-Mart's Vudu. Of these, Netflix is by far the most popular, with over 40 million subscribers worldwide. If you're one among those millions, you're likely to want Netflix on your Fire TV. Use these steps to install Netflix:

1, At the Home Screen, scroll down to Apps and

select it.
2. Scroll to the right, highlight the Netflix icon (shown below), and press Enter. In a moment, you will see the app screen for Netflix.

Select Netflix icon.

The app screen for a selected app shows any cost for the app (free in the case of Netflix), overviews, and reviews from users.

3. Use your remote to highlight the Download icon and select it.

4. The 'Download' option changes to a 'Downloading' icon, and finally to an 'Open' option. Click Open, and the Netflix app will launch.

Assuming you are a Netflix member, you can enter your email address in the space provided, and then enter your Netflix password. You can use the navigation pad on your fire TV remote to select the characters needed to enter your password. Remember that you can press the !#$ key to enter special characters, if these are part of your password.

Once you've installed the app, it appears under the apps category on Fire TV, under the Your Apps subcategory. It also appears in the Recent subcategory when Home is selected within the main menu. At any time, you can select either option to begin watching Netflix.

Mirroring your Kindle Fire to your Big-Screen TV

You can "mirror" all more recent models of Kindle Fire tablets to many TV sets, including most smart" TVs, any streaming device using the Miracast standard, and any TV equipped with Amazon Fire TV or Amazon Fire TV Stick. Mirroring takes any display that you see on a Fire tablet, along with any audio, and reproduces it at your TV. The Fire tablet must be a model produced after September 2012 (a "3rd generation" or "4th generation" model).

Before you mirror the screen of your Fire tablet, ensure your TV or media streaming device is turned on and "discoverable," meaning that your Fire tablet can locate and connect to your device using your Wi-Fi network. With Amazon Fire TV or Fire TV Stick, scroll down the main menu of Fire TV and select the 'Settings' option, then choose 'Display and Sounds,' and at the next screen select 'Enable Display Mirroring.' With "smart" TVs or TVs equipped with Miracast streaming devices, refer to the user guide for your TV or streaming device for the exact steps needed to make your device "discoverable."

Once your hardware (on the "TV" side of the equation) is ready, you can mirror your Fire display with these steps:

> 1. Swipe down from the top of the screen of your Fire to open Quick Settings.
>
> 2. Tap Settings.
>
> 3. Tap Display and Sounds.
>
> 4. Tap Display Mirroring. Your Fire tablet will now display all compatible devices within wireless range.
>
> 5. Find your TV or streaming device within the list and tap the device name to connect.

Note that the initial connection may take as long as 30 seconds. If your Fire tablet is able to mirror the display and audio on the other device, you'll see "Mirroring" beneath your device name. You can tap Stop Mirroring to stop mirroring the screen of your Fire.

TIP: In the author's experience, mirroring can be finicky. On at least two occasions, I've been unable to successfully connect, and both devices were Amazon products (a Fire HDX 8.9 and both a Fire TV console and a Fire TV Stick). If you are unable to mirror on the first attempt, try rebooting both your Fire tablet and the streaming device or smart TV. (If you are using Fire TV or Fire TV Stick, unplug the power cord from the Fire TV device, turn the TV off and on, and re-connect power to the Fire TV console or stick.) After rebooting both devices, you will again need to make your smart TV or streaming device "discoverable."

Using the Parental Controls feature of Fire TV Stick

If you have young ones in your household, you'll probably want to enable the parental controls feature of your Fire TV Stick. Parental controls will allow you to prevent purchases and restrict any access to Amazon content including movies, TV shows, games, apps, and photos. You can enable parental controls using the following steps:

1. At the Home screen, choose Settings, then choose Parental Controls.

2. Using the Fire TV remote, press the select button to turn on Parental Controls.

3. Enter your Parental Controls PIN, and then choose Next. (Your Parental Controls PIN is the same PIN that you use

for all of your Amazon services such as Amazon Instant Video.)

After you set up your Parental Controls PIN, you can change any of the following settings:

- Require your PIN for all purchases
- Require your PIN for Amazon instant video only
- Block the ability to view or purchase certain content types such as games or apps
- Change your Parental Controls PIN

Once you enable parental controls with your Fire TV Stick, most actions related to viewing of content, purchasing content, or changing settings will require you to re-enter your Parental Controls PIN.

Note that the parental controls feature restricts access to Amazon content, but does not restrict any content provided by other apps (such as Netflix). If you allow unrestricted use of Fire TV apps, you'll need to check your installed apps for any parental control options provided by that app. In Netflix, you can enable Netflix Parental Controls by editing your Netflix profile; log into your Netflix account in a web browser and see the Netflix Help Center for details.

Installing and Using the Fire TV Remote App

In addition to controlling your Fire TV Stick with the Fire TV Remote or with an optional Amazon Game Controller, you can also control your Fire TV Stick using a Fire HD or HDX tablet, a Fire Phone, and most Android devices (the device must be running Android version 4.0 or higher). You can use any of these devices as a remote by downloading and installing the Fire TV Remote App. To download the Fire TV Remote App, go to the Amazon or Android Appstore from your Fire tablet, Fire Phone, or compatible Android device and search for "Fire TV Remote App." When you locate the app, tap the "Download" or "Install" button, and follow the instructions displayed on your screen to complete the installation.

Before using the app as a remote, you will need to pair the app with your Fire TV Stick. Ensure that your tablet or phone and your Fire TV Stick are connected to the same Wi-Fi network. Launch the app, and in the list of devices that appears, select your Fire TV Stick by name. In a few moments, a code will appear on your TV screen. Enter this code in the text box in the app to complete the pairing of your device with your Fire TV Stick.

Once your tablet or phone has been paired with your Fire TV Stick, you can launch the app at any time and use it as a remote control for your Fire TV. The following tables list the actions that you can take on the screen of your tablet or phone.

Navigate menu items and categories	To move the selection… - **Up**: Swipe from the middle to the top - **Down**: Swipe from the middle to the bottom - **Left**: Swipe from the middle to the left - **Right**: Swipe from the middle to the right - **Scroll**: Swipe and hold to a specific direction
Use navigation options:  **Home**  **Menu**  **Back**	At the bottom of the screen, tap any of the navigation icons.

Access media controls: 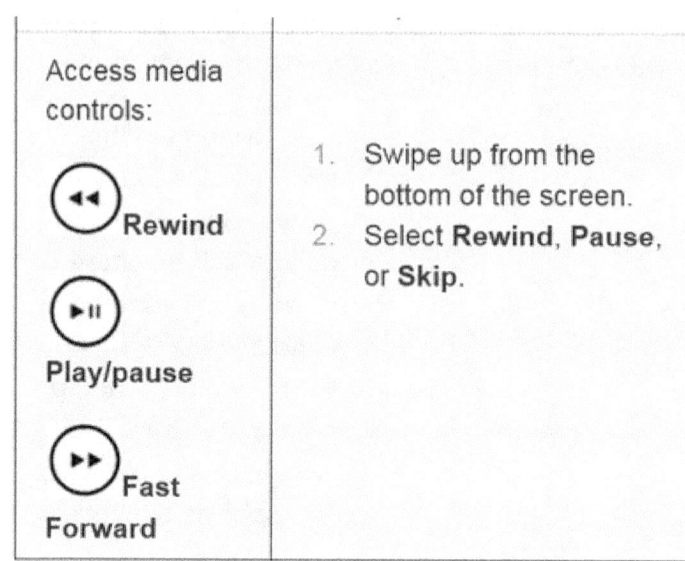 Rewind Play/pause Fast Forward	1. Swipe up from the bottom of the screen. 2. Select **Rewind**, **Pause**, or **Skip**.
Enter text with a keyboard	1. Select the keyboard icon in the top right corner of the screen. 2. Enter text. 3. Tap **Done** to close the keyboard.

Note that when you pair a Fire TV Remote App with your Fire TV Stick, you cannot unpair it. (You can reset your Fire TV Stick, in which case all paired devices will be removed.)

About Amazon Prime & Amazon Prime Instant Video

If you are a major fan of watching movies and television shows and are based in the US, the author has a recommendation for you. Consider becoming a member of Amazon Prime, if you aren't already a member. For an annual fee of under $100 (at the time of this writing), in addition to the free two day shipping on a variety of items, you will also get to watch thousands of movies and shows from the Amazon Prime video library on your Fire TV Stick at no cost. Prime members can also stream movies and shows, and if you also own a Kindle Fire HDX tablet, you can download Amazon Prime movies and watch them offline later (truly a frequent flier's dream). Note that due to licensing restrictions placed on Amazon by content providers, Amazon Instant Video is not available outside the US and Puerto Rico at the time of this writing.

Your yearly subscription to Amazon Prime includes free unlimited access to thousands of movies and TV shows from Amazon Prime Instant Video, part of Amazon's own video streaming service. Note that there is Amazon Prime Instant Video and there is Amazon Instant Video, and the two aren't exactly the same. Amazon Instant Video is Amazon's video streaming service, with tens of thousands of movies and TV shows available for rent or purchase at various prices. Amazon Prime Instant Video is the library of all Amazon Instant Video content that happens to be free to Amazon Prime members. You can tell whether a video is free with your Prime membership by looking for the "Prime" banner at the upper-left corner, as shown in the following example:

To quickly browse what's available when you're a Prime member, first choose a category of Movies or TV from the Main Menu of the Home Screen. Then scroll to a Prime-related subcategory—Recently Added to Prime, Top Movies on Prime, or Kids Movies on Prime (for movies), or Top TV on Prime and Kids TV on Prime (for TV shows). Once you have a subcategory selected, you can use the left and right portions of the circular trackpad on the remote to scroll within the displayed results. Find a movie or TV show you want to watch, press the center of the trackpad to select it, and press the center of the trackpad once more to begin watching.

One disadvantage in comparison to Netflix: Amazon Instant Video provides access to thousands of movies, but they generally are not newly released movies. If you're looking for the latest theatrical releases as soon as they are available by way of streaming or on DVD, you're more likely to find these at another pay streaming provider such as Netflix or Hulu plus.

To buy or not to buy, that is the question...
When using the Amazon Instant Video store as a source for your movies and TV shows, you'll need to make a decision as to whether you want to buy or rent the movie or TV show in question. Video rentals are available for a

set period of time, typically three days. The clock starts running on this time period when you begin watching the rental for the first time. You can watch the rental as many times as you wish during the rental time period.

Movies and TV shows that you buy can be viewed at any time. These are stored in the Amazon Cloud, so they are always just a tap away from viewing. Rentals of entire series of TV shows are not typically available, so if you want to watch the entire series of a TV show, you will need to buy the series unless it's available on Amazon Prime Instant Video and you are a Prime member. If this is the case, you can watch any episode in the series for free using your Prime membership.

Make your desired selection-- purchase or rental-- at the bottom of the screen when the video is displayed. If you are a Prime member and if the video is available through Amazon Prime, the first button on the left will display "Watch Now Amazon Prime." Successive buttons will display "Buy" or "Rental" choices, assuming rentals are available. (Note that some movies can only be purchased and are not available as rentals.) Select the desired button to process your purchase or rental and begin watching your movie or TV show.

The Murky Practice of 'Geo-dodging'

There are major restrictions on where content produced in the US can be viewed, and this applies not just to Amazon Instant Video, but also to other major content providers such as Netflix, Hulu, and Crackle. Viewers in the United States have what basically amounts to unrestricted access to American content provider offerings, such as Amazon Prime Instant Video, Netflix, and Hulu. Unfortunately, this is not the case for many overseas viewers. Overseas viewers typically face licensing restrictions that prevent the sale or rental of many American shows overseas. (In some cases, the restrictions work the other way around; the phenomenally popular iBBC player used by so many to watch shows in the United Kingdom cannot be legally downloaded in the United States.)

There are ways around these problems, but before you non-US viewers get too excited, you should know that there are a number of technical and legal issues that make this a technically complex and legally gray area. A practice known as "geo-dodging' is gaining popularity, particularly in Britain, Australia, Canada, and Germany, as well as within communities where a large number of American "expats" are based, such as Dubai, Saudi Arabia and other parts of the middle east, Tokyo, and Hong Kong. Geo-dodging is a practice whereby certain techniques and software (apps) are used to circumvent restrictions placed on geographical locations outside the United States by content providers.

DISCLAIMER: Absolutely no endorsement, actual or implied, should be inferred from any mention of techniques or software services throughout the remainder of this subheading. Geo-dodging is a murky area as far as the law is concerned, and many of the practices involved fall into violation of the terms of service of the major content providers.

Those who have used the techniques behind geo-dodging will readily admit that the primary path to success lies simply in knowing how to pay for your desired content. US-based content providers typically require that your account use an email address provider in the United

States, and that your purchases be billed to a credit card issued from a US-based bank. Geo-dodgers often set up separate content provider accounts using legitimate US based mailing addresses (some have been known to use the address of a stateside Starbucks). They set up an account with a content provider, then add a cash value to the account using US gift cards or a bank card payment made by a friend or relative residing in the US. A number of streaming services in the US also accept US-based PayPal accounts, although geo-dodgers still report a need to associate a valid US credit card with the PayPal account.

Causing a US-based content provider to assume that an overseas resident appears to be based in the US for billing purposes is only half the battle, according to geo-dodgers. The geo-dodgers report that the other half of the battle amounts to convincing the content provider that the purchaser is actually based in the US (meaning, the Internet traffic comes from a US-based IP address). This is often accomplished with the use of a proxy server or a virtual private network, configured to imitate a device having a US IP address. Browser-based plugins, such as FoxyProxy and Proxy Switchy, and VPNs (virtual private networks) such as HotSpot Shield, VPNBook, and WiTopia offer servers in the large cities of the US, as well as many different nations overseas.

Proxy wars between the dodgers and the providers have also inspired a rise in DNS-based geo-dodging services. These services simply change the DNS address (which is admittedly something that a tech savvy user could accomplish on their own). Services like Unblock US and UnoTelly will route your outbound Internet traffic through a US-based DNS address for a monthly fee. And if you will be happy with web browser access via a Firefox or Chrome browser installation, many dodgers are happy with the free Hola plug-in for Firefox or Chrome. The plug-in provides access to a free DNS-based geo-dodging service that works with major content providers.

It's important to note that content providers are cracking down on many virtual private network service providers and proxy servers by banning the IP addresses belonging to these organizations, so it's important to realize that what works today in terms of geo-dodging may not work tomorrow. It's a constantly shifting landscape, with content providers on one side and the virtual private networks and proxy servers used by the geo-dodgers on the other.

Coming soon: Amazon FreeTime for Fire TV Stick

If you happen to own a Kindle Fire HD or HDX, and you have young ones in your household, chances are that you know about FreeTime. FreeTime gives children restricted access to your content. FreeTime not only lets you limit the types of content young ones can watch, it also lets you establish time limits that specify the hours that young ones are allowed to watch television. At the time of this writing, FreeTime is not available for Fire TV Stick. However, Amazon has announced that an upcoming software update will include FreeTime for Fire TV. If you're interested, check the website www.amazon.com/FireTV for additional details.

Tip: Keep your kids entertainment safe. If you have young ones around your house, you'll want to enable parental controls for the Fire TV Stick. With parental controls turned on, you can set up a five digit pin and block certain content- including movies, TV, and games- and no purchases can be made without your pin. At the Home Screen, go to Settings > Parental controls, and turn parental controls on. You will be asked to create a five digit pin, and once you do this, there will be additional items that you can manage to determine what your young ones can (and cannot) watch.

Chapter 4 - Playing games with Fire TV Stick

This chapter examines the gaming features of Fire TV Stick. Amazon's Fire TV was the first major streaming device designed to handle gaming, and Fire TV Stick continues that tradition. As mentioned in Chapter 1, the hardware crammed into the small footprint that is the Fire TV Stick provides reasonable performance, in the view of many casual game players. (If you are expecting Fire TV Stick to rival a Microsoft X-Box or a Sony PlayStation in terms of game-playing performance, you will be sorely disappointed; there's a reason that those platforms retail for roughly ten times the cost of a Fire TV Stick.)

Amazon also offers an optional dedicated Game Controller, priced around $40 US at the time of this writing. The Fire TV Game Controller has a natural, solid fit in your hands, especially when compared to the rather massive controller that ships with Microsoft's X-Box. (You can also play games that are compatible with Fire TV Stick using the remote control that ships with Fire TV Stick.)

As for the games themselves, Fire TV Stick has current game offerings that include Disney's Toy Story, Pixar's Monsters University, Sonic the Hedgehog 2, the Game of Life, You Don't Know Jack, and many more. A major benefit of the Fire TV Stick as a game platform is the reasonable cost of games; many games are free, and the average cost of a Fire TV Stick game is less than two dollars US per game.

Which Controller?

Before using your Fire TV Stick as a gaming platform, you'll need to decide which controller you prefer to use. Games can be played using the Fire TV Stick remote control, or with the optional Game Controller. However, not all games are compatible with both controllers. Some games require the use of the Fire TV Stick remote control, others require the Game Controller, and still others can be played using either controller. To determine which controllers are compatible with a particular game, navigate to the game, then select the More Info button. Next, you'll see an overview page for the game. Look for the "Works With" section, and you'll find the controller information in this area.

Pairing additional Game Controllers

By default, Fire TV Stick uses the Fire TV remote control as a Game Controller. If you purchase an optional Game Controller for your Fire TV Stick, you will need to pair the Game Controller with your Fire TV Stick. Use the following steps to pair a Game Controller with your Fire TV Stick:

1. If your Game Controller is fresh out of the box, install two AA batteries in the underside of the unit, as shown in the following illustration.

2. At the Home Screen, select Settings, then scroll to the right and select Controllers.

3. To add a Game Controller, select Bluetooth Gamepads. (If you want to add a second Fire TV remote, select Amazon Fire TV Remotes.)

4. Press and hold the Home button on your Game Controller (or remote) for five seconds.

5. Choose the new Game Controller or remote from the list of discovered devices, using your Fire TV remote that is currently paired to your Fire TV Stick.

Playing games

Starting a game is a simple matter. (Playing a game with any level of skill may be another matter entirely, but these directions will get you underway!) At the main menu of the Home Screen, select Games. Next, choose an existing game from your games library (if you've downloaded any games). You can also browse among popular lists or spotlight items, or you can select categories, then highlight a given category to browse all the available games within that category.

Once you've located a desired game, highlight the game and press the Select button on the Fire TV remote (or the "A" button on the Game Controller). You'll be taken to an overview screen that shows details of the game, including any costs involved in purchasing the game. (Note that you must have Amazon 1-Click ordering turned on to download games, even in cases where the game is free.)

To install the game, highlight the "Buy" button then press "A" on the Game Controller (or press 'Select' on the Fire TV remote). The button on your TV screen will change appearance to read "Download" as the game downloads, followed by "Installing" as the game is loaded into the system memory of the Fire TV Stick. Once the button changes to display "Open," you can select the button to start the game.

Navigating with the Game Controller

The optional Game Controller has a number of controls that are not found on the Fire TV remote, and the purchase of the controls differ from game to game. The illustration that follows shows the overall uses for the controls of the optional Game Controller:

- ① Left analog stick / L3 button
- ② D-pad
- ③ System/navigation buttons (back, home, menu)
- ④ GameCircle button
- ⑤ Media control buttons (rewind, play/pause, forward)
- ⑥ Right analog stick / R3 button
- ⑦ Input buttons (A, B, X, Y)
- ⑧ R1 shoulder button
- ⑨ L1 shoulder button
- ⑩ R2 trigger
- ⑪ L2 trigger
- ⑫ Four lighted player number indicators
- ⑬ Battery door

Uninstalling games

At times, you may wish to uninstall games from your Fire TV Stick. There are two very valid reasons for doing this: first, so the appearance of your Home Screen is not cluttered with games that you are no longer using, and secondly, to save space in memory so that you can install more games!

Games are loaded into flash memory that is built into your Fire TV Stick, and there is a limit to the amount of flash memory available. The Fire TV Stick is equipped with 8 GB of memory. This sounds like plenty, but some games (especially those with multiple characters, detailed graphics, and layers upon layers of role-play) can consume large amounts of memory.

You can check the available memory space at any time by going to the Home Screen and choosing Settings. Select System, then About, and you'll see the storage capacity, both in terms of what is used and what is available.

To uninstall a game that you are no longer using, select Games in the main menu, go to Your Games Library, and highlight the game that is no longer wanted. With the game highlighted, select the Uninstall button, and the game will be uninstalled, freeing the memory space.

About Amazon GameCircle

Amazon GameCircle improves your gaming experience by saving your achievements, high scores, and time played to the Amazon Cloud, so you can compare your progress and skills with friends and other GameCircle members. Fire TV Stick supports GameCircle, which was originally developed for the Kindle Fire line of tablets. GameCircle can be thought of as a gamers' social sharing network, with access built into the Kindle Fire HD, the Kindle Fire HDX, and Fire TV.

With GameCircle, players can track their accomplishments and see how many badges they've earned. Leaderboards give players an easy way to compare their scores to the competition. (The first of two illustrations that follow shows an example of accomplishments of a group of friends, while the second shows a leaderboard for a particular game.)

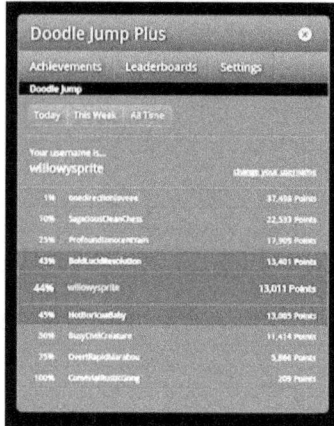

Games that have been written to support GameCircle provide Sync options, which let players store their game progress to the Amazon Cloud. This makes switching between devices in midstream a no-brainer. As an example, you could stop a game on Fire TV Stick and resume gameplay at the point where you left off on a Kindle Fire HDX).

Games that have been written to work with GameCircle will automatically enable GameCircle when the game is loaded. When you launch such a game, you will see a "welcome back" message near the bottom of the screen. Press the Home button on your Fire TV Stick remote, OR press the GameCircle button on the Game Controller.

The exact screen that you will see next will vary, but in every case you will see a screen with details about your GameCircle profile. You'll see options for displaying achievements and leaderboards, as well as a summary of your game's progress.

Changing your GameCircle Profile

In GameCircle, every game player has a profile, which is hidden from others by default. If you want to share your accomplishments with other gamers, you will need to make your profile visible. To do this, at the Fire TV Stick Main Menu, select Games, then press the Menu key on either controller (it's the button with three horizontal bars). A Game Profile screen appears, where you can change your nickname (the name that is visible to your GameCircle friends), and you can also select a GameCircle picture for your profile. Make your entries and choose "Save and Continue" to store your profile information and return to your game.

Hiding Your GameCircle Profile

You can hide your gaming information from the GameCircle network of gamers. Note that when your profile is hidden, you cannot send or receive friend requests, or view other users' profiles. To hide your profile, at the Home screen, choose Settings > Applications, and then select Amazon GameCircle. Finally, choose Share your GameCircle Nickname so that the feature is turned Off.

Ten Games worth considering for Fire TV Stick

We will close out this chapter with a brief listing of games that you may wish to add to the lineup of your Fire TV Stick. Games are an admittedly subjective area, and as a new gaming platform, the game marketplace for Fire TV Stick is quickly growing. At the time of initial product launch, slightly over 200 games were available for Fire TV Stick, and game developers are known to be hard at work on many more.

Fibbage, by Jackbox Games

Fibbage is a great party game from the same company that brought you the game "You Don't Know Jack", and how well you will play the game depends significantly on whether you can tell a "fib" (or to be honest, how well you can lie) with a straight face. A quick rundown of the game is this: you and other players in turn are asked a question, and everyone is given a certain amount of time for typing a lie and for filling in the blanks. The lies are then added to the multiple-choice answers, and you have to choose the right answer. You get points when people choose your lie, and you lose points when people choose someone else's lies.

This is a great one for two to eight people gathered around the Fire TV. The free version does have a limited set of questions, but it is upgradable to a full version that has a much more comprehensive set of questions.

You Don't Know Jack, by Jackbox Games

You Don't Know Jack is one outstanding game show/ trivia style party game. As the game makers state, this is a comedy / trivia style game where high culture and pop culture collide. Covering everything from "sharks" to "sharts", You Don't Know Jack is the only trivia game that will have you laughing and thinking at the same time, and sometimes vomiting a little. The questions are all timed, and you get more points for answering faster. At the same time, you are penalized for providing wrong answers.

This game has been around for years, and is a fun game to play with family and friends, mostly due to the hilarious questions and answers. The free app does have a limited pool of questions, and if you play it often, you will want to upgrade to the full version which has a much more complete set of questions and answers.

Flappy Bird, by Dotgears

Flappy Bird consistently gets 4 to 5 stars for subjecting its users to a love/hate relationship with a video game. This game can be super-addictive, frustrating, enjoyable, maddening, and entertaining at the same time. If you are a fan of the SuperMario style of games of the 80s and 90s, you will love this one. New features have been added to this version, which was engineered especially for FireTV and the FireTV Stick. These features include a two player mode that lets you challenge your friends, the ability to share your best score, and more obstacles that make the game even harder than with previous editions.

Zen Pinball HD, by Zen Studios

Zen Pinball HD is a virtual pinball machine that gets high marks for its realism and gameplay. The game was engineered for great performance on mobile devices, and features an outstanding selection of pinball tables, including the critically acclaimed 'Marvel pinball' series.

The game itself is a free download, and the popular "Sorcerers Lair" pinball table is included. Note that you will have to pay additional fees if you want to download other pinball tables. If you grew up with pinball machines, you're sure to find Zen Pinball HD to be one viciously addictive game.

Tetris, by Tetris Online, Inc.

What can we say about this one? Tetris is Tetris, and unless you've been living in a cave for the last 20 years or you were born after this one's popularity faded, you probably have a good idea of how Tetris works. For those who aren't aware of the concept, Tetris presents you with a series of shapes made up of blocks, falling from the sky. As each block falls, you must rotate the block so that when it lands, it fits neatly into an existing row of blocks. As the game progresses, the blocks fall faster and faster until it's extremely challenging at best to prevent the screen from filling with blocks (and when the screen does fill, it's game over).

This variation of the game by Tetris Online, Inc is not free (cost is $2.99 at the time of this writing), but this implementation of Tetris is one of the better ones on the market, thanks to its variety of levels. You can test your skills in any of three different game modes (Marathon, Sprint, or Ultra) and there are over 40 different achievements that you will encounter along the way. If you are a member of Amazon GameCircle, you can also compare your scores against other GameCircle members.

Monsters University by Disney

Monsters University answers the question, "what videogame costs just $.99, works with the Fire TV Stick remote, and is fun for the entire family?" Based on the Disney / Pixar film Monsters University, the game lets you play as one of your favorite characters from the film, and rack up points for being the scariest monster on campus.

NOTE: This app contains in-app purchasing, which allows you to buy items using actual money. If Fire TV Stick is shared by young ones in your home, you may want to activate Parental Controls to prevent unauthorized purchases. To do this, go to the Settings menu and select Parental Controls. Also, note that this app does contain links that will allow you to connect with others by means of social media.

Sonic the Hedgehog 2 by SEGA

For all of you pre-millennials (children of the 90s) out there, one of the great hits of the videogame universe has been digitally re-mastered for Fire TV Stick. Go back in time to the days of the Sega Genesis, and re-discover the game that united Sonic the Hedgehog with his flying sidekick Miles "Tails" Power. As the game player, you'll speed through loops and jump across hundreds of barriers in a race to take out the evil Dr. Eggman.

SEGA has reengineered this version exclusively for Amazon devices, and the redone game features in-game content and re-mastered audio while staying true to the original concepts of the game. Sonic the Hedgehog 2 does require the use of the optional Game Controller.

Bingo Blitz by Buffalo Studios, LLC

A detailed tutorial isn't needed for most Fire TV Stick owners for this one, after all, its bingo, played much the way bingo has been played for five centuries. Technology has done away with the paper-based variety and has added slots, at least in this version, called Bingo Blitz. Hangout in any one of over 50 captivating rooms, including 30 with exotic international themes. Bingo Blitz adds arcade style gameplay to create a more addictive game of bingo.

Bingo Blitz also supports a real-time multiplayer experience. You can connect and play against thousands of players around the globe, and chat real time with other bingo players online. Bingo Blitz can be played with the Fire TV Stick remote or with the Game Controller. *NOTE:*

This app contains in-app purchasing, which allows you to buy items using actual money. If Fire TV Stick is shared by young ones in your home, you may want to activate Parental Controls to prevent unauthorized purchases. To do this, go to the Settings menu and select Parental Controls.

The Game of LIFE by Electronic Arts

The classic board game is translated into digital format in this Electronic Arts adaptation of The Game of LIFE. While remaining true to the overall style of play, you will enjoy sound and visual effects, music, and eye-catching landscapes. You may only live once in real life, but in The Game of LIFE, you get to live again and again, and have fun and hopefully, learn a few things about life along the way.

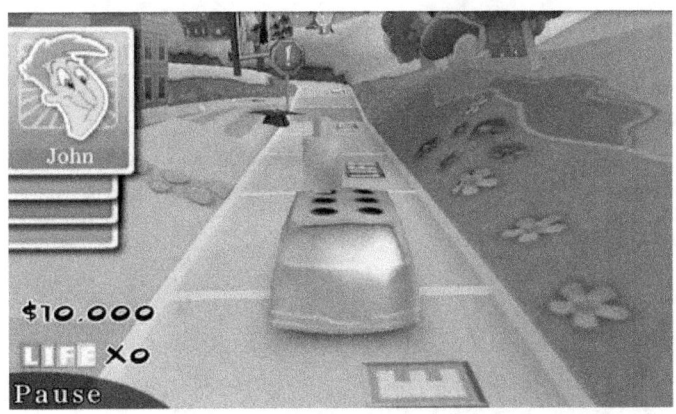

Despicable Me: Minion Rush by Gameloft

Gru's minions face a serious challenge in this game based on the popular movie Despicable Me. As a player, you play as a minion and compete with the other minions in a number of comical challenges, all in an attempt to impress ex-super villain Gru (who happens to be your boss). Fly, jump, avoid obstacles, capture bananas, get into mischief, and defeat other minions to earn the "Minion of the Year" award.

NOTE: This app contains in-app purchasing, which allows you to buy items using actual money. If Fire TV Stick is shared by young ones in your home, you may want to activate Parental Controls to prevent unauthorized purchases. To do this, go to the Settings menu and select Parental Controls.

Chapter 5 - Apps you should have in your Fire TV library

(Image courtesy Amazon, Inc.)

In this chapter, we fill you in on twenty top rated apps that you want to consider installing in your Fire TV library. Most of these apps provide content from a variety of sources other than Amazon Instant Video. If you have purchased the optional Voice Search remote, keep in mind that the voice search feature of Fire TV does not work with most apps. With the exception of Hulu Plus, which does provide limited voice search capabilities, you'll need to perform searches within the app itself using the keyboard methods described by the app itself, when searching for content.

1. Netflix

Netflix is the number one streaming provider in North America, offering thousands of movies and TV shows to its members. At the time of this writing, membership costs $9.99 monthly to new subscribers. In return for the monthly charge, you get unlimited movies and TV shows that are commercial free. The app may be free, but of course you'll need a Netflix subscription to actually watch any content. Given that fact, if you are a Netflix subscriber, you'll want the free Netflix app for your Fire TV library. You can watch all of the same Netflix videos that you might see streamed to your laptop, and you can enjoy that Dolby surround sound which comes across nicely if you connect a surround-sound system to your large-screen TV. Log into the app with your Netflix account, and you can get their usual unlimited shows and flicks through your Fire TV Stick, and can even pick up where you left off on a show you'd started watching earlier on your TV set or on a portable device such as a smartphone or a Kindle Fire tablet.

One major limitation of Netflix on Amazon Fire TV is that the Fire TV voice search is not supported (at the time of this writing). This means that if Netflix has a movie that subscribers can view for free and Amazon Instant Video has the same movie as a $2.99 rental, if you perform a voice search, you see only the Amazon Instant Video listing; the Netflix listing does not appear. (Netflix has stated that the company expects to build in support for Fire TV Stick Voice Search by the end of the year. Until that happens, to search Netflix for content, you must resort to the tedious and awkward on-screen keyboard.)

Also keep in mind that multiple family members can also log into Netflix using the same account. If your household includes young ones, you may wish to enable the parental controls that are built into Netflix.

2. Hulu Plus

This is another case where the app is free, the service isn't, but it can be well worth the monthly subscription cost. With Hulu Plus, you get unlimited streaming of hundreds of current hit TV shows, as well as critically acclaimed movies. (Unlike Netflix, Hulu Plus does include a limited number of commercials.) The current shows include ones like Modern Family, Desperate Housewives, The X-Files, Law and Order Special Victims Unit, and The Daily Show with John Stewart. Classics include past episodes of Lost, Family Guy, Battlestar Galactica, and more. Being multiplatform, you can watch your Hulu Plus-supplied content on your Fire TV library, as well as on Microsoft XBox 360 or Xbox One or your Sony PlayStation 3 or Playstation 4. At the time of this writing, unlimited streaming will run you $7.99 per month, but you can sign up for a trial subscription for free.

Hulu Plus lacks the incredible variety of Netflix; however, you will find movies and shows on one that are not on the other. So if you're a serious fan of movies and television, you may want to consider subscribing to both services.

3. Crackle

Often referred to as "the poor man's Netflix," Crackle is an outstanding source of FREE (that's correct, as in 'no subscriber or pay-per-view fees involved) movies and TV shows. With the Crackle app installed on your Fire TV library, you get immediate access to thousands of full-length Hollywood movies and TV shows. Crackle is owned by Sony, so much of the content you will see comes from the archives of Sony Pictures or Sony Television. At the time this was written, the lineup on Crackle included movies like Pineapple Express, Big Daddy, Joe Dirt, Mr. Deeds, Alien Hunter, The Deep, Panic Room, S.W.A.T., and hundreds of others. Also in the Crackle lineup are dozens of TV shows like Seinfeld, The Prisoner, Marvel Comics' Iron Man animated series, All in the Family, and Chosen, just to name a few. Twenty new movies and TV episodes are added to the lineup each month, from genres that include action, anime, comedy, crime, horror, thrillers, and sci-fi.

The available content is far less than you'll find on Netflix or Hulu Plus, and you must endure commercials, but the price is right. Crackle is also beginning to carry some original content not found elsewhere, such as Jerry Seinfeld's new show, "Comedians in cars getting coffee." Crackle is truly free internet entertainment at its best, so given the non-existent cost, you should definitely have the Crackle app as one of your apps.

4. Pandora

Pandora Internet Radio lets you create a personalized radio station that's based on your favorite artists and your favorite songs. You tell Pandora about the songs, artists, or genres you are fond of, and Pandora does the rest, producing a stream of music that is geared to your tastes. You can give each song that plays a "thumbs up" or "thumbs down" rating. (A "thumbs down" rating ensures that the song in question will never again be played on a Pandora playlist that is associated with your login.)

Pandora on the Fire TV library offers the same capability as the Pandora app that runs on most smartphones and tablets: the ability to create personalized radio stations based on your favorite artists and songs. If you are already a Pandora user, you can just log into Pandora on Fire TV Stick and pull up your same stations that you've set up on your desktop or laptop PC, Kindle Fire or other tablet, or smartphone. The interface is a breeze to use, and you can view artist biographies. Pandora is an ad-supported service, so you will hear ads on your stations; however, you can opt to purchase the Pandora One subscription for $3.99 per month and get ad-free listening.

A NOTE OF CAUTION: The Pandora app does let you buy digital content, which gets billed to the credit card that is linked to your Amazon account. If other family members share the use of your Fire TV Stick, you'll probably want to set up parental controls to prevent unintentional spending.

5. iHeart Radio

iHeartRadio is a free, all in one digital radio service that lets you find stations that already stream via the Internet, or create your own favorite all music custom stations based on your artists listening preferences. Over 1500 stations are available from around the country, spanning the range of pop, rock, R&B, country, hip-hop, urban contemporary, college radio, and talk stations. You can browse by music genre, or go to a geographical location and then hit the 'scan' button to jump from station to station in that area. The choices of available stations is not as comprehensive as is TuneIn Radio with over 100,000 stations. However, both apps are free, and each has stations that the other lacks, so consider installing both to ensure that your favorite radio stations will be available.

The number one complaint about the app from reviewers is that it uses the Facebook user verification plug-in to allow saving of custom play lists or custom station lists. So if you want to save anything in this program, you will need to have a Facebook account.

6. Showtime Anytime

If you already subscribe to Showtime through your cable or satellite provider, you can use the Showtime Anytime app to stream all of Showtime's offerings to your Fire TV library. Catch any of the first run movies that Showtime is known for, as well as on demand access to Showtime original series that include Dexter, Homeland, and House of Lies.

The app is free, but you must be a valid subscriber of Showtime to view the content. You will be asked to login once with your username and password for your cable or satellite TV provider. Authorized providers include AT&T U-verse, Bright House Networks, Comcast, Cox, Dish Networks, Google Fiber, Time Warner Cable, and Verizon FIOS.

7. Movies by Flixter

For the movie buff who wants to stay abreast of all the latest movie theatrical releases, DVD releases, and reviews, Movies by Flixter is the app to have. You can scroll and browse through new releases and box office favorites, and you can view showtimes in your area and even order tickets! If you are a Netflix subscriber, you can log into Netflix from the Movies by Flixter app, and add movies to your watchlist within Netflix.

8. Plex

Plex is a media streaming app that lets you stream all of your personal media (no matter where they are stored), so you can enjoy those media files on any of your devices including the TV set that's attached to your Fire TV library. Stream personal videos, photos, and music on your personal computer to your Fire TV library screen, or to your android-based smart phone or tablet. (The personal computer must be running Plex Media Server, which is a free download at https://plex.tv).

9. WatchESPN

This free app lets you catch the best of ESPN, right on your Fire TV library screen. Along with live games and studio shows, you also get 24 / 7 access to ESPN, ESPN2, ESPN3, ESPNNews, and ESPN Deportes. In the WatchESPN lineup, you will find all of the following:

- NFL Monday night football
- NBA regular-season and playoffs
- Major League Baseball
- US Open
- The Masters
- The Open Championship
- College football and college basketball
- Grand Slam tennis events

You'll also get regular sports news, commentary, and analysis, including shows like SportsCenter, Game Day, and SportsNation.

The app is free, but you must be a valid subscriber of ESPN to view the content. You will be asked to login once with your username and password for your cable or satellite TV provider. Authorized providers include AT&T U-verse, Bright House Networks, Comcast, Cox, Dish Networks, Google Fiber, Time Warner Cable, and Verizon FIOS.

10. Bloomberg TV

You'll find the top stories of the world of business on Bloomberg TV. This live, 24 hour global business and financial news channel covers the most important stories in the business world. Shows on Bloomberg TV lean heavily towards topics that would appeal to an investor, and most shows include a five minute review of where the global stock and bond markets are trending every 30 minutes. In addition to the markets, other show topics cover subjects such as technology, travel, automotive, and luxury items. And a weekday show called "Bloomberg West" does an outstanding job of covering the latest technology developments from a Silicon Valley perspective.

11. VEVO

VEVO is the largest collection of online music videos. You can view the latest new music videos, catch live performances by your favorite artists, and create playlists that feature your favorite artists. VEVO sources an online music catalog that includes 75,000 videos by over 21,000 artists, and VEVO also provides a small amount of original music programming. The service is free and you're not required to create a login account but if you choose to do so, you'll be able to share your favorite videos with your Facebook and Twitter friends. VEVO is advertiser supported, so you will need to endure small ads that appear prior to the start of some of the videos.

12. TuneIn Radio

This streaming radio app lets you tune in to any of over 100,000 commercial radio stations and over 2 million radio programs that you can listen to on demand. Catch favorite shows and radio personalities live, browse among thousands of stations according to format (news, weather, talk, sports, pop, country, urban, R&B, religious), and tune in to critically acclaimed national networks that include BBC, NPR, TEDTalks, and more. You can also create your own customized music stations with content based on the artists that you choose.

13. Frequency

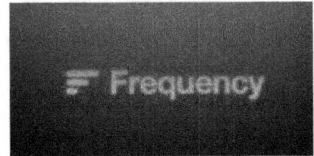

Frequency is an aggregator, meaning it finds and collects video clips of subjects that interest you from all over the web and gives you a single place to view all of your favorite videos. Instead of bouncing around between Facebook, YouTube, twitter, CNN, and a half dozen of your favorite blogs, you can let Frequency find and organize your favorite videos into streaming channels.

14. HuffPost Live

HuffPost Live is a streaming video network with content based on the popular online resource The Huffington Post. What makes HuffPost Live different from other online resources is that HuffPost Live lets you (and other viewers) become a part of the conversation. HuffPost live uses stories from the Huffington Post as a starting point for conversations that occur in real-time, with viewers playing the role of on-air guests. The topics covered are as varied as those covered by the Huffington Post website itself, from financial news, political analysis, hot topics (race relations, gay rights, gun control) to celebrities and entertainment, and everything in between.

15. Red Bull TV

Red Bull TV is a streaming service specializing in extreme sports. Brought to you by Red Bull, the popular energy drink maker, Red Bull TV features shows whose topics include motorsports, off-roading, snowmobiling, aircraft racing, paragliding, surfing, and more. You can view a show that's dedicated to a specific extreme sport, or you can watch hour-long blocks of assorted videos that come from a variety of extreme sports playgrounds. If you crave breathtaking shows crammed with adventure and excitement, Red Bull TV is a channel you should have on your Fire TV library.

16. RealPlayer Cloud

RealPlayer Cloud is a cloud (or Internet)-based storage solution that lets you watch, store, and share your personal videos across all devices. It is available as a free app for Fire TV Stick, and RealPlayer Cloud apps are also available for Apple IOS devices (MacBooks, iPads, iPhones); android-based tablets including Amazon's Kindle Fire line, most smartphones, and Microsoft Windows platforms including PCs and Microsoft Surface tablets. With RealPlayer cloud, you can share your videos across all of your devices, and you can share them with friends.

One of the most impressive features of RealPlayer Cloud is that you don't need to worry about converting videos into some specific file format before you can share that video. RealPlayer Cloud uses its own patented SurePlay technology to automatically format videos for the screen size, resolution, and bandwidth of the playback device. With SurePlay, the video just plays using the best quality possible, no matter what device you're using to play your video.

Signing up for RealPlayer Cloud is free, and all you will need to supply is a username, a valid email address, and a response to a few generic questions such as your gender, month and year of birth, and ZIP Code. You'll get 2 GB of storage space for free, and you can add massively to that amount by enrolling in a paid subscription plan (the author is currently paying roughly 5 dollars monthly for 25

GB of storage). You can find more details about RealPlayer Cloud at www.real.com.

17. Vimeo by Vimeo

vimeo

Vimeo is a video-sharing website that makes it easy for users to upload, share, and view videos. With the Vimeo app for Fire TV Stick, you can view a variety of videos by top video creators from all over the globe. You can view Staff Picks and add videos to a Watch List where you can watch them later.

Using a computer, smartphone, or tablet, Vimeo also lets you create and upload your own videos. If you're interested in creating and uploading your own videos (which you can then view on your Fire TV Stick), learn more and sign up for a free Vimeo account at www.vimeo.com.

18. Portfolio for OneDrive by Snapwood Apps

Portfolio for OneDrive is a photo gallery and uploader designed to work with Microsoft's OneDrive cloud storage solution. You can view full-screen slideshows for a single album or for multiple albums, and you can batch upload multiple photos at a time to OneDrive.

19. tinyCam Monitor Pro for IP Cam

tinyCam Monitor Pro is an app that can be used with wireless IP cameras for security monitoring, baby monitoring, and video surveillance. Monitor private or public IP cameras directly from Fire TV Stick to keep track of your baby, pet, home, business, traffic, and weather. tinyCam Monitor Pro supports the MJPEG and MPEG/H264 video standards used by the major webcam vendors.

20. YouTube

The YouTube app is available for Fire TV. You can use the app to browse or search for any one of hundreds of thousands of videos on the YouTube site. Basically, this app links to YouTube's mobile optimized website. While the app does as advertised, giving you access to YouTube, be warned that because voice search does not work inside of apps at the time of this writing, searching is an incredibly torturous process.

Tip: Send YouTube videos from your tablet or phone to Fire TV Stick. As mentioned above, using the hunt and peck method of entering a search string into the YouTube app for Fire TV Stick is painful, to say the least. An alternative is to stream YouTube videos from your android phone or your iPhone directly to the Fire TV Stick. Open the YouTube app on your android phone or iPhone, and begin displaying the YouTube video of your choice. When you do this, you should see a cast icon underneath the video. When you tap on that icon, another window will appear displaying "Connect to device." This window will list all available devices that can be connected, including your Fire TV Stick. Select your Fire TV Stick by name to display the YouTube video.

Chapter 6 - It's your life: photos, personal videos, and music

A major plus of Amazon Fire TV Stick over its' competition is that Fire TV Stick provides an easy solution to the problem of how to display your family photos and movies on your big screen TV. For many, it's always been a bit of a technical hassle to play local content-- local meaning photos and video files stored on your desktops, laptops, tablets, and smartphones scattered around your house. Fire TV Stick overcomes this difficulty, allowing you to easily stream your personal photos and videos simply by uploading them to your Amazon Cloud Drive account.

Amazon Cloud Drive is just one example of cloud-based storage, which greatly increases your possible maximum storage space by saving data to web servers that reside on the Internet. (Other cloud-based storage solutions that cater to consumers include Google Drive, Microsoft OneDrive, and Real Player Cloud.) A major advantage of using Amazon Cloud Drive for storing your photos and personal videos is that your photos and videos are synchronized across all your devices once you install the Cloud Drive app on each device. The Amazon Cloud Drive app is available for most consumer devices, including Apple and Windows computers, and Android, Windows, and Apple IOS-based tablets (including the Kindle Fire HD and HDX) and smartphones.

Installing Amazon Cloud Drive on your computer, tablet, or smartphone

If you are using a laptop or a desktop (Windows or Mac), just point a web browser at the following address:

http://www.amazon.com/gp/drive/app-download

The site will automatically detect the version needed for your computer and operating system, and it will present you with a download option. Download and run the installation file. You will be asked to sign into your Amazon account if you're not already signed in.

Once you've installed the app, you can launch it and easily upload your photos to the Amazon Cloud Drive using the drag and drop interface. When you launch Amazon Cloud Drive on a desktop or a laptop, the app will be intuitively familiar in appearance and operation, as it bears an uncanny resemblance to the file manager of your computer (File Explorer under Windows, or Finder under Apple Mac). The following illustration shows an example of Amazon Cloud Drive running on a Windows laptop.

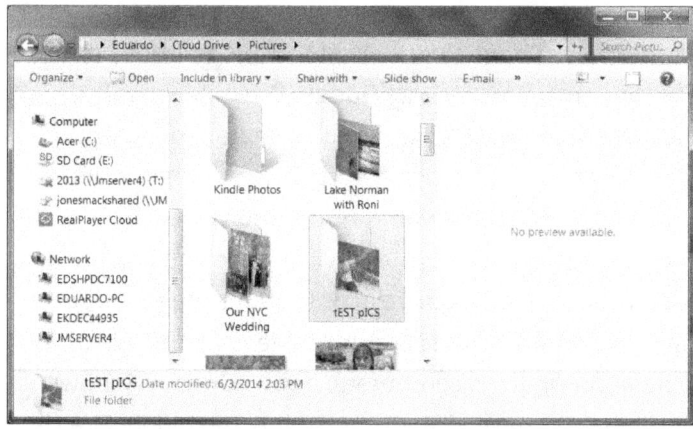

To upload photos or videos, just open a folder containing the desired picture or video file, and drag it to the Amazon Cloud Drive window. If you drop the file into a folder within the CloudDrive window, the photo or video will appear within that folder under Photos on Fire TV Stick.

Tip: Use your smart phone or tablet, it's so simple!

For smart phones and tablets running Android, Windows, or Apple's iOS, placing your photos in the Amazon Cloud Drive is even easier: once you install the app, all you have to do is take a picture, and your phone or tablet does the rest! Go to the App Store for your particular phone and search for Amazon Cloud drive photos. Install the app, and sign in with your Amazon account and password. You will see a message indicating that autosave is turned on (the default). Tap OK to accept the setting, and you are done!

From this point on, any picture you take using the smartphone or tablet will automatically be saved to your Amazon Cloud Drive account (and available for viewing on your Fire TV Stick).

Viewing your photos and videos

After you've uploaded your photos or videos to your Amazon Cloud Drive account, you can view them on Fire TV. Scroll down the Fire TV main menu, and select Photos. When you do so, all of your photos and personal videos will appear on the screen in a tile-based layout, similar to the example shown in the following illustration.

You can scroll through and select any photo to display it on your TV screen. In the case of personal videos, pressing the select button will trigger the play arrow in the center of the video, and the video will begin playback. You can use the fast-forward, rewind, and play / pause buttons on your Fire TV remote to navigate through the video.

Organizing your photos into albums

When you have any number of photos, the Photos category of the Home Screen will become unwieldy in terms of visual clutter. To avoid this, you will want to organize your photos into albums. This is also a simple task, because any folders that you create in the Amazon Cloud Drive window will appear as Albums under the Photos menu of Fire TV Stick. Simply click the "New Folder" button at the top of the Cloud Drive window, and when the new folder appears, type a name for the folder. The folder will appear as an album under your Fire TV Stick Photos, and all pictures that you drag into that folder will appear under that album.

Tip: You can have folders within a folder (which appear within Fire TV Stick as albums within an album). For example, you might create a folder titled "Vacation Photos" and you might then create three folders inside that folder, titled "Carnival cruise 2012," "London trip 2013," and "Our visit to Grandma." Each of the subfolders would contain the pictures associated with that folder's topic, helping you to better organize your photos.

Creating slideshows and screensavers

The photos menu option of Fire TV Stick has a slideshow feature that lets you play slideshows of your photos, and you can also select any photos to serve as your Fire TV Stick screen saver. Using your remote, select Photos from the main menu and highlight the desired photo. Once a photo is highlighted, you will see two buttons beneath the photo: "Start slideshow" and "Set as screensaver." If you select start slideshow, every photo in that folder on your cloud drive will be displayed in successive order. If you choose "Set as screensaver, that particular photo will be used as your screensaver (the image that appears when Fire TV Stick has been inactive for a set period of time.

The Amazon Cloud Drive account provides you with 5 GB of storage space, which is roughly enough to store over 2200 average photos. Since the Amazon Cloud Drive account costs you nothing with a 5 GB allotment, it is well worth your taking the time to install and use the Amazon Cloud Drive app.

Playing music from your Music Library

If you have music files or music purchases stored in the Amazon cloud, you can play your music using Fire TV. (You can't purchase or upload music using Fire TV, but you can add to your music library using the Amazon Music App running on any compatible PC, Android, or iOS device.) Use these steps to play music on your Fire TV:

1. At the Home screen, choose Music.

2. Browse for music in the Recently Played list, Playlists, Artists, Albums, or Genres. If you have added a Prime Playlist to your Music Library, you will also be able to browse by Prime Playlists.

3. Select a playlist, artist, album, or song to start playing. Use the playback controls on the remote or the Fire TV Remote App to play, pause, forward, or rewind the music

NOTE: To stream Amazon Music, your Fire TV Stick must be authorized to your Amazon account. You can have up to 10 devices authorized to your account, and each device

can only be authorized to one Amazon Music account at a time.

tip! Import your iTunes, Microsoft Zune, or other music library into your Amazon Cloud account using the Amazon Cloud Player. If you have an Amazon account, you already have storage space for your existing music files in the Amazon Cloud. Amazon has an easy to use tool that makes importing your iTunes or other music library a simple matter. Open a browser window on your computer, and visit http://www.amazon.com/cloudplayer (if you are in North America) or visit http://www.amazon.co.uk/cloudplayer (if you are in the United Kingdom) and set up a CloudPlayer account. Once you set up an account, click the Import Music button at the upper left, and follow the directions that appear on the screen. After you've imported your songs into the Amazon Cloud Player, those songs will appear under the "Music" heading at the Home screen within Fire TV.

Chapter 7 - Sideloading Apps

While it is true that developers are working hard behind the scenes to bring more apps to the Amazon AppStore, the fact remains that thousands of Android apps—often available through the Google PlayStore—are simply not certified for the Amazon Fire products (Fire Phone, Fire TV, and Fire HD and HDX tablets). This is unfortunate, because an estimated 75% of all Android apps will run, unmodified, on a Fire Phone or Fire tablet, and a smaller yet still significant number will run under Fire TV.

There is a solution to this problem, although it involves a moderate level of "geek skills" and is definitely not for the faint-of-heart. (This book may have been titled "made easy," but there is nothing admittedly 'easy' about the topic of this final chapter, and it is understandable if you prefer to skip this sort of technique entirely.) The process is called sideloading, and it involves downloading the APK file from a source other than the Amazon AppStore and manually installing the app. ("APK" flies are Android Application Packages, files in a special file format that are used to install software on devices that run Google's Android operating system.)

DISCLAIMER: Before proceeding, be aware of the fact that sideloading requires a moderate amount of technical skills. You will need to know how to install 3rd-party applications on your desktop or laptop computer (Windows or Apple iOS-based), and you will need to know how to run software from a command prompt. Secondly, finding 3rd-party Android apps that will operate on a Fire TV can be challenging, due to the differences between traditional Android devices and Fire TV. Fire TV lacks a touchscreen, keyboard, accelerometer or *gyroscope, so apps that make use of any of these components will not run properly under Fire TV.*

The major drawback to the practice of sideloading is that sideloaded apps are not coming from a trusted source, Apps supplied by the Amazon AppStore have passed quality control checks at Amazon, while random apps that you find all over the Internet have **not** passed any quality control testing by Amazon. You greatly increase your chances of infecting your device with a virus or other malware when you sideload Android apps to your Fire device.

Downloaading and installing apps by sideloading

If your eyes haven't glazed over just yet; you can use the following steps to sideload an app onto Fire TV.

---

1. On a separate computer in the same network, Install and setup Android Debug Bridge (ADB). The Android Debug Bridge is a set of tools used by developers to create Android apps, and you can find a simple one-step installation and complete instructions for downloading and installing the Android Debug Bridge Stand-Alone Installer courtesy of the folks at Sourceforge.net by going to the following website:

http://sourceforge.net/projects/adbstandalone/

Download the ADB Stand Alone installer file from Sourceforge.net, and run the install to install ADB on your computer.

2. On your Fire TV, scroll down the Main Menu and select Settings, then System, then Developer Options.

3. Turn on the 'Enable ADB Debugging' option and the 'Apps from Unknown Sources' option.

4. Using Fire TV's menu, choose Settings,–> System –> About –> Network.

5. Locate the entry labelled 'IP Address' within the dialog that appears. This will be a sequence of numbers, typically in the format of 192.168.0.xxx (as an example, my master bedroom Fire TV was assigned an address of 192.168.0.10, while my living room Fire TV Stick was assigned an address of 192.168.0.19).

6. At your desktop or laptop computer, get to a command prompt (on a Windows machine, you can click Start and enter 'cmd' in the Run a program box). The first command line that you need to enter is as follows:

cd\adb

This assumes that you installed the ADB program in a default directory. If you installed it elsewhere, you'll need to use the command prompt CD\ command to change to the directory where you installed the adb program.

7. Using file management techniques, copy the APK file for the app that you wish to sideload into this same directory.

8. Within the same command prompt window as was used earlier, enter the following:

adb start-server

(and note the presence of the hyphen between the words 'start' and 'server')

9. In the same command prompt window, enter the following command:

adb connect 192.168.1.xxx

-where 'xxx' matches the actual IP address for your Fire TV. In a moment, you should see a "connected to..."confirmation message. If you see an "unable to connect..." message, make sure that your computer and your Fire TV are both located on the same network, and that you performed Step 3 of this process.

> 9. Finally, within the same command prompt window, enter the following command:

adb install <apk filename>

-where <apk filename> is the name of your APK file, such as, ***adb install my_screen_saver.apk***. The APK file will be installed on your Fire TV. **This process will take anywhere from a few seconds to a few minutes, depending on the size of the APK file and your home network speed. During this time, you will see no indication of progress other than a blinking cursor in the command prompt window.** When the installation process has completed, a message will appear in the command prompt window indicating that the APK file has been installed on your FireTV.

> 10. If you have additional apps to sideload, repeat Step 9 for each app. When you are done sideloading apps, in the command prompt window, enter the command ***adb kill-server*** followed by the command **exit** to close the window. (It is probably a wise idea to reverse the settings you changed in Step 3 back to "Off" to maintain system security from possible viruses and malware.)

So, where's my app?

After going through all the necessary work to setup the ADB package on your computer and install the APK flle on your Fire TV, you go to the Home screen, only to discover that there's no sign of the app! Don't panic; this is by design. Amazon controls the apps that are allowed to appear on the Home screen, and sideloaded apps that you've found outside the Amazon Apstore do *not* fall into the 'Amazon-approved' category.

To access your sideloaded apps, simply scroll down within the main menu to Settings, then scroll over to Applications. Once inside the Applications category, select 'Manage all installed applications.' You will see a list of all your installed apps similar to the example shown.

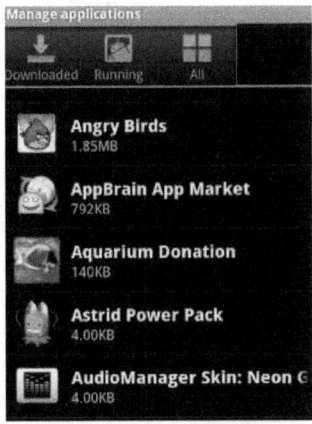

Scroll through the list until you locate the name of your sideloaded app, and select the app to run it.

Where do I find apps worth sideloading?

Asking the above question is somewhat similar to asking "where can I buy stuff online," but we'll try to offer a start. ApkApps, at apkapps.com/apps is one source, and Sourceforge.net is another. Wherever you choose to look for apps worth sideloading to your Fire TV, check the app permission levels to try to ensure that the app is not overly intrusive, and read the user reviews (where provided) to guard against malicious apps.

Chapter 8 - Basic troubleshooting tips for Amazon Fire TV Stick

In the complex world that is high-technology, things don't always go smoothly. This chapter provides a list of common problems that may arise with Fire TV Stick, and possible solutions for those problems.

Difficulty with purchasing or accessing your content	Make sure that your Fire TV Stick has a valid connection to the Internet. An Internet connection is necessary to stream, purchase, or synchronize any content. You can verify that you do indeed have a valid Internet connection by going to your Home Screen, and choosing Settings > System > Wi-Fi. Also verify that your Amazon 1-Click payment method is properly set up. You must have a 1-Click payment method set up with your Amazon account in order to purchase any content, even if the "purchase" is free.
Movies, photos, or other purchased content does not appear on your Fire TV Stick Home Screen	Check to make sure your Fire TV Stick is registered to the correct Amazon account. Go to the Home Screen, choose Settings, and then choose My Account. If the wrong account is shown, select the account by name, then select Deregister. Finally, choose Register and enter the information requested to register the proper Amazon account.
Cannot connect to a Wi-Fi connection	If your Fire TV Stick is unable to connect properly to a Wi-Fi connection, there are a number of things that could cause this issue. Check the following:

	Your Fire TV Stick should be connected to one of the following types of networks or routers: Open, WEP, WPA/WPA2, PSK, and WPA/WPA2 / EAP encrypted networks
	If you've never been able to connect to your home network, make sure you are using a compatible Wi-Fi router. These include type B, G, and N routers at 2.4 GHz and A and N routers at 5 GHz.
	Make sure that wireless connectivity has been enabled on your Fire TV Stick. Go to the Home Screen, choose Settings > System > Wi-Fi, and verify that the wireless setting is set to ON.
	Verify that your Home Wi-Fi network has not dropped off line. Many issues with a home Wi-Fi network can be solved by restarting the router or cable modem.
	Try restarting the Fire TV Stick. To do this, unplug the power cord from the wall outlet, wait five seconds, and reinsert the power cord.
The remote control does not operate	If your remote control suddenly stops working, there are a number of steps that you can take to troubleshoot the problem. 1. Make sure that the batteries are inserted correctly, and if it has been a while since you changed them, replace the batteries. 2. Reboot the Fire TV Stick. To do this, disconnect the power cord, wait five seconds, and reconnect the power cord. 3. Make sure that the upper left corner of the remote is not covered or obstructed in any way, because the antenna is located in this area and the remote will not work properly if the antenna is covered.

	4. Re-pair the remote to the Fire TV Stick. To do this, wait until the Home Screen is completely displayed, then press and hold the Home button on the remote for 10 seconds. The remote should automatically pair with the Fire TV Stick console and you should see a message on the screen indicating that the remote has successfully paired.

Amazon Fire TV Stick Troubleshooting Help Video

You may wish to refer to the Troubleshooting video provided by Amazon for general Fire TV Stick troubleshooting tips. Point a web browser at www.amazon.com/help and at the page that appears, click "Fire, Kindle and Echo" on the left, then click "Fire TV Stick" on the right. At the next screen, under "Fire TV Basics," click "Fire TV Help Videos." When the "Basics" video begins playing, pause it and scroll down and tap on the "Troubleshooting" link to play the Troubleshooting video.

CONCLUSION (and a favor to ask!)

I truly hope that you enjoy using Fire TV Stick as much as I have enjoyed both using and writing about both Fire TV Stick and its heavyweight big brother, Fire TV. As an author, I'd love to ask a favor: if you have the time, please consider writing a short review of this book. Honest reviews help me to write better books. You can post a review by going to the book's web page at Amazom.com (at the site, do a search on 'fire tv stick Edward jones'). When the page appears, click the page to open it, scroll down to the bottom of the page and click the "Write a customer review" button. And my sincere thanks for your time!

-Ed Jones

Other Books by Edward Jones

Both 'Kindle Fire Tips, Tricks and Traps' books are available at Amazon in print or electronic editions.)

Kindle Fire HDX Tips, Tricks, and Traps: A Tutorial for the Kindle Fire HDX. If you happen to own BOTH a Kindle Fire HDX, and a Kindle Fire HD, you may already know that they are *not* the same device. In this comprehensive guide, you'll learn tips (ways to effectively use your Kindle Fire), tricks (ways to improve the operation of your Kindle Fire), and traps (things to avoid to prevent problems while using your Kindle Fire). Learn to use features that are new to the HDX line, including Google or Outlook Calendar and Contacts synchronization, Microsoft Exchange corporate e-mail support, and Amazon's 'Mayday' online technical support. This book also details how you can use the built-in cameras (front-facing in the 7-inch model, front-and-rear facing in the 8.9-inch model) to take photos and videos; how you can setup the security options to protect your account information; and how you can provide a safe environment for children using parental controls and Kindle FreeTime. If you own a Kindle Fire HDX, you owe it to yourself to get the book that's been written *exclusively* for the **Kindle Fire HDX**!

For your Kindle Fire HD, get Kindle Fire HD Tips, Triks, and Traps, the book that covers the design and features of ALL models in the Fire HD product line! Many books about the Kindle Fire HD do NOT apply to the Kindle Fire HD currently shipping from Amazon. THIS BOOK has been written to cover BOTH the current ("4TH and 3rd generation") Kindle Fire HD, AND the earlier ("2nd and 1st Generation") Kindle Fire HD.

If you are looking for a top-notch tutorial at a reasonable cost, you've come to the right place! This is the book that will teach you 100% of what you need to know. Kindle Fire HD Tips, Tricks, and Traps: A How-To Tutorial for the Kindle Fire HD is your detailed guide to getting the maximum benefit from your Kindle Fire HD.

Top 300 Free Apps for the Kindle Fire is your guide to 300 of the top rated apps that you'll find useful for your Kindle Fire. Jones has taken the time to research and compile this extensive list of apps for your Kindle Fire, and best of all, each of these apps are FREE. You'll find apps for the home office, for entertainment, for news, weather, and sports, for your health, for managing your finances, for playing games, and more. A local news apps section provides news, weather, and traffic apps for over 50 major US cities, and a travel section gives you an insight to the best apps that will help you find great deals on flights, hotel rooms, cruises, dining, and even the best gas prices around your hometown or when on the road. Each listing begins with a clickable link back to the Amazon catalog. So as you read the electronic version of this book on your Fire tablet, if any particular app sounds like what you've been looking for, just tap the image or heading name. You'll be taken directly to the Amazon page for the app, where you can click the button to install that app. (Active wi-fi connection required.) Let Top 300 Free Apps for the Kindle Fire be your guide to the best free apps for your new tablet!

For a complete listing of my books, see my Author page on Amazon at-

amazon.com/author/edwardjones_writer

Join our mailing list...

We would be honored to add your name to our mailing list, where we can keep you informed of any book updates and of additional tips or topics about the Kindle Fire, Fire TV Stick, and any future hardware-related products from Amazon. Our mailing list will NEVER be sold to others (because we hate spam as much as you probably do), and the only information that we will ask you to supply is a valid e-mail address. Go to-

>www.thekindlewizard.com

>-and click the 'Sign up for our newsletter' link.

"Fire TV Stick Made Easy" print edition © 2 December 2014 by Jones-Mack Technology Services of Charlotte, NC.

Digital rights provided by agreement to Amazon Digital Services, Inc.

Amazon, Fire TV Stick, Kindle, Kindle Fire, the Amazon Kindle logo and the Kindle Fire logo are trademarks of Amazon.com, Inc. or its affiliates.

No part of this book may be reproduced, stored within a retrieval system, or transmitted without the express permission of the publisher. All rights reserved.

www.ingramcontent.com/pod-product-compliance
Lightning Source LLC
Chambersburg PA
CBHW051722170526
45167CB00002B/768